AF504039
GARfield
Jim Davis

This edition first published by Ravette Publishing in 2008.

Ravette Publishing Limited
Unit 3, Tristar Centre,
Star Road, Partridge Green,
West Sussex RH13 8RA

ISBN: 978-1-84161-306-2

IN HIS SECOND

COLOUR COLLECTION

JIM DAVIS

RAVETTE PUBLISHING

gARFIELD

·CLICK·

TAPPY TAPPY
TYPE TYPE TAPPY
TAPPY
TYPE

·CLICK·

YOUR ORDER HAS BEEN
PROCESSED. THANK YOU

"WWW.DINGLEBALL.COM"?
JIM DAVIS 7-30

IT'S THE CROWN PRINCE OF LAZINESS!

ALL HAIL HIS HIGHNESS, PRINCE FAT SLOB!

OFF WITH HIS MOUTH!
JIM DAVIS 7-31

THERE ARE DAYS WHEN I JUST DON'T FEEL LIKE DOING ANYTHING. TAKE TODAY FOR INSTANCE...

JIM DAVIS 8-1

GARFIELD, ALL YOU EVER DO IS SLEEP

WHAT IF THE WHOLE WORLD WERE LIKE YOU?

WE'D BE A POOR, YET RESTED, PEOPLE
JIM DAVIS 8-2

HI, I'M A WORM

I BURROW UNDER THE GROUND AND EAT DIRT
WHAT DO YOU DO FOR FUN?

I LIKE TO BOOGIE DOWN ON THE SIDEWALK AFTER A GOOD RAIN
JIM DAVIS 8-3

DO YOU LIKE BEING A WORM?

DO CATS EAT WORMS?
NO

I LOVE BEING A WORM
JIM DAVIS 8-4

SO, YOU LIVE UNDERGROUND AND EAT SOIL?
THAT'S RIGHT

WHAT DO YOU DO FOR A LIVING?
DIG

THAT'S NOT TOO GLAMOROUS
IT PUTS DIRT ON THE TABLE
JIM DAVIS 8-5

Garfield

BOY, IT'S A SCORCHER TODAY!
IT SURE IS

YOU LOOK LIKE YOU COULD USE A BREAK FROM THE HEAT, PAL...

NOOO, NO... YOU'RE JUST A MIRAGE. YOU CAN'T BE REAL

YOU'LL NEVER KNOW FOR SURE UNLESS YOU HAVE A LITTLE TASTE

C'MON, YOU KNOW YOU WANT ME...
JIM DAVIS 8-6

HE'S LICKING YOUR LAWN ORNAMENT?

GARFIELD, IS THIS YOUR COFFEE OR MINE?

SIP

MINE

YIP! YIP! YAP! YAP! YAP! YIP!

YIP! YAP! YIP! YAP! YAP! YIP! YAP! YIP!

THAT'S TELLING IT

I THINK I PULLED A MUSCLE IN MY PINKY FINGER WHILE TRIMMING THE BOUGAINVILLAEA

WELL, IT HURTS!
STAND BACK, EVERYONE... GIVE THIS MAN SOME AIR...THE AMBULANCE IS ON ITS WAY...

YOU IRK ME
JIM DAVIS 8-10

DICTIONARY

THANK YOU!

I SAW A WOMAN AT THE MALL TODAY WITH A BIG TATTOO OF A BOWLING BALL ON HER LEG
JIM DAVIS 8-11

SHE WORE AN EYE PATCH, AND WAS CARRYING AN IGUANA

YOU ASKED HER OUT, DIDN'T YOU?
SHOT ME DOWN LIKE A ONE-WINGED DUCK

AHHH...THAT WAS A GREAT MEAL, WASN'T IT?

WHAT?...OH YEAH, SURE

SLUP
SLUP
SLUP
SLUP
THAT BOY LOVES HIS PIZZA
PIZZA
JIM DAVIS 8-12

GARFIELD

I'M A FLY
SO I SEE

I HAVE WINGS AND YOU DON'T. I CAN FLY AND YOU CAN'T

I CAN WALK ON THE CEILING AND YOU CAN'T

I HAVE COMPOUND EYES MADE UP OF HUNDREDS OF HEXAGONALLY-FITTING FACETS, AND

SMACK

WITH ALL THOSE EYES, YOU'D HAVE THOUGHT HE WOULD HAVE SEEN THAT COMING
JIM DAViS 8-13

I WAS A LONELY CHILD, GARFIELD
HO BOY...
JIM DAVIS 8-14

MY PLAYMATES WERE BARNYARD ANIMALS

EVER TRY TO GET A HEIFER INTO A TREE HOUSE?
LET'S NOT GO THERE

URSUELLA NELSON...MY FIRST GIRLFRIEND
PHOTOS

WE HAD SOME WILD TIMES
PHOTOS

AT NIGHT WE'D SNEAK OUT TO THE BARN AND DRINK UNPASTEURIZED MILK!
ANOTHER PIECE OF THE PUZZLE
PHOTOS
JIM DAVIS 8-15

I'M NOT A COUNTRY BOY ANYMORE, MOM
JIM DAVIS 8-16

I EVEN BUY EGGS AT A STORE

DON'T CRY, MA!
YOU COULD HAVE BROKEN IT TO HER MORE GENTLY

I REMEMBER SUMMER NIGHTS ON THE FARM...

A GENTLE BREEZE WAFTING THROUGH THE MEADOW...

CHASING EACH OTHER WITH CATTLE PRODS...
THERE WAS SOMETHING IN THE WATER

HERE'S A GREAT PICTURE FROM THE FARM
PHOTOS

IT WAS TAKEN THE DAY WE GOT INDOOR PLUMBING
PHOTOS

THE ENTIRE FAMILY GATHERED AROUND THE TOILET
YOUR MOM LOOKS SO PROUD CUTTING THAT RIBBON
PHOTOS

I WASN'T A POPULAR CHILD, GARFIELD
GO FIGURE

THE OTHER KIDS WOULD GO OUT AND PLAY "JUMP ROPE"

WHEN I CAME OUT, IT WAS "TIE THE GEEK TO A TREE"
HEY, THEY INCLUDED YOU

GARFIELD

JIM DAVIS 8-20

ALL RIGHT, THAT WAS
THREE TIMES...NOW
LIE DOWN!

BRING MY PANTS BACK!

SLAP!
SLAP!

AAIIIIIEEEE

NOTHING LIKE A LITTLE AFTERSHAVE LOTION TO HELP YOU FIND THAT PAPER CUT

I FINALLY GOT THE TOILET UNCLOGGED

KNOW WHAT IT WAS?

WELL?!
HE WAS HAVING A DRINK, AND I WAS IN A PLAYFUL MOOD...

WHIRRRRRRRRRR
THAT'S IT, JONNY BOY...THAT'S IT!
JIM DAVIS 8-24

WHIRRRRRRRRR
MAKE THAT BABY WHINE!

WHIRRRRRRRRRR
ATTA BABY! ATTA BABY!
CAT FO
GARFIELD
www.garfield.com

DING-DONG
© 2000 PAWS, INC./Distributed by Universal Press Syndicate

YAAAHHHH!
www.garfield.com

YOUR DATE'S HERE
JIM DAVIS 8-25

IT'S SO SAD THAT YOU DON'T KNOW HOW TO SHARE
© 2000 PAWS, INC./Distributed by Universal Press Syndicate

SAD FOR YOU, MAYBE
www.garfield.com
JIM DAVIS 8-26

GARFIELD

BAY-
BEE!
BAY-
BEE!

YES, YES, YES, YES,
YESSSSSSS!
© 2000 PAWS, INC./Distributed by Universal Press Syndicate

HOO!
HOO!
HOO!
HOO!

THUMP!
THUMP!
THUMP!
THUMP!

HOO DA MAN?!
HOO DA MAN?!
YOU DA
MAN
JIM DAVIS 8-27

PAPER SAYS THERE'S AN ICE AGE COMING
JIM DAVIS 8-28

IT'LL BE HERE IN TWO MILLION YEARS
© 2000 PAWS, INC./Distributed by Universal Press Syndicate

BETTER START MOVING TO THE CELLAR, GARFIELD...
HA, HA, HA
www.garfield.com

SAYS HERE THEY DISCOVERED AN ANCIENT CITY
© 2000 PAWS, INC./Distributed by Universal Press Syndicate

MAYBE SOMEDAY THEY'LL FIND THIS HOUSE!

WONDER WHAT THEY'LL SAY
"ARCHAEOLOGIST FINDS BAD SUIT"
www.garfield.com
JIM DAVIS 8-29

© 2000 PAWS, INC./Distributed by Universal Press Syndicate

I'M STILL HERE

I CAN READ VERY SLOWLY
I CAN SIT FOR A LONG TIME
www.garfield.com
JIM DAVIS 8-30

I SAW A BEAUTIFUL WOMAN ON THE BUS YESTERDAY, GARFIELD

IT WAS LOVE AT FIRST SIGHT

AT LEAST ON MY PART
"WOMAN JUMPS FROM MOVING BUS"
JIM DAVIS 8-31

WHEN I'M DONE WITH THE PAPER, I'LL FIX YOUR DINNER
JIM DAVIS 9-1

RIP RIP
RIP RIP RIP
RIP RIP
RIP RIP RIP
RIP

AS SOON AS I SAID THAT, I KNEW IT WAS A MISTAKE
YOU'RE DONE WITH THE PAPER. NOW, FIX MY DINNER!

THERE ARE A LOT OF PROBLEMS IN THE WORLD

SOME OF WHICH AREN'T YOUR FAULT

RARE PRAISE INDEED
JIM DAVIS 9-2

GARFIELD
JIM DAVIS 9-3

!

TAP
TAP
SCARY
STORIES
II

HELP! I'M A JELLY-FILLED DONUT!
JIM DAVIS 9-4
www.garfield.com

I'M AFRAID SOMEONE WILL EAT ME!

WILL YOU PROTECT ME?
SOME DAYS, LIFE KISSES YOU RIGHT ON THE LIPS
© 2000 PAWS, INC./Distributed by Universal Press Syndicate

I'M HOT
JIM DAVIS 9-5
www.garfield.com

I'M HOT

HOT'S TAKEN. YOU'LL HAVE TO BE COLD
© 2000 PAWS, INC./Distributed by Universal Press Syndicate

THE LAST COOKIE IS GONE
JIM DAVIS 9-6
www.garfield.com

AND I THINK IT'S SAFE TO ASSUME WHERE IT WENT
DON'T BE TOO SURE...
© 2000 PAWS, INC./Distributed by Universal Press Syndicate

I'M NOT THE ONE WITH CHOCOLATE CHIPS ON MY TONGUE

www.coffeequick.com
TIC TIC TIC!

CLICK
DING-DONG

I NOW OFFICIALLY LOVE THE INTERNET
JIM DAVIS 9-7

BUT WHY WON'T YOU GO OUT WITH ME, BETH?!
JIM DAVIS 9-8

I CAN'T DANCE?! WELL, I CAN DANCE!

I'M DOING A BOX STEP WITH MY CAT RIGHT NOW!
WHY DO YOU ALWAYS HAVE TO LEAD?

BOY, IT'S HOT!

CLOP CLOP CLOP

AND WE'RE SHORT ON ICE CUBE TRAYS!
JIM DAVIS 9-9

GARFIELD

JIM DAVIS 9-10

COOTCHIE, COOTCHIE, COO!

YOU CAN'T STAY ON THE CEILING FOREVER
JIM DAVIS 9-11

I ATE A MILLIPEDE FOR LUNCH
JIM DAVIS 9-12

HOW WAS IT?
AWFUL!

HE WENT DOWN KICKING AND SCREAMING AND KICKING AND SCREAMING AND KICKING...

JIM DAVIS 9-13

SWAT SWAT SWAT SWAT SWAT SWAT

THAT WAS SOME IMPRESSIVE OPEN-FIELD RUNNING
THANK YOU

MY UNCLE BARTON WAS AN ACTOR

HE DIED TRAGICALLY WHILE SHOOTING A BUG SPRAY COMMERCIAL

THEY GAVE HIM A UNION FUNERAL... OPEN COCOON, 21-FLY SALUTE... EVERYTHING
YOU'RE BORING ME
JIM DAVIS 9-14

DID YOU SQUISH MY HUSBAND YESTERDAY?!
PROBABLY

THEN I NEED YOU TO SIGN THESE INSURANCE PAPERS VERIFYING HE WASN'T INJURED ON THE JOB
WHAT WAS HIS JOB?

HOUSEHOLD PEST
THEN HE WAS ON THE CLOCK, LADY
JIM DAVIS 9-15

WOULD YOU LIKE TO HEAR THE STORY OF MY LIFE?
SURE

SMACK

KEEP IT SHORT!
JIM DAVIS 9-16

GARFIELD

JALAPEÑO!

CAYENNE!

HABANERO!

PERUVIAN DEATH PEPPER!

FOOM

YOU WIN...
THEN WHY AM I NOT HAPPY?
JIM DAVIS 9-17

YOU'RE READING?

INSTEAD OF PAYING ATTENTION TO ME?!

HERE'S AN ARTICLE ABOUT YOU
I CAN WAIT
JIM DAVIS 9·18
www.garfield.com

THE DOG SAYS, "ARF"
JIM DAVIS 9·19

THE COW SAYS, "MOO"

AND THE CAT SAYS,...
LEAVE ME ALONE OR I'LL BITE YOUR BOOK
www.garfield.com

HE JUST KEEPS ON READING

TOTALLY IGNORING MY NEEDS
JIM DAVIS 9·20

FORCING ME TO PULL ONE OF THOSE LITTLE HAIRS OUT OF HIS NECK
www.garfield.com

WOULDN'T IT BE GREAT TO WALK ON THE MOON, GARFIELD?

OH, I SEE RIGHT THROUGH YOUR THINLY VEILED PLOY, PAL...

ALWAYS TRYING TO GET ME TO EXERCISE!
JIM DAVIS 9-21

"A RUBBER MOUSE CAN PROVIDE HOURS OF ENTERTAINMENT FOR YOUR CAT"
JIM DAVIS 9-22

WHICH REMINDS ME...

WHERE'S YOURS?
MELTED IT DOWN. MADE EARPLUGS

JON LEARNS A WORD EVERY DAY

HERE'S A GOOD ONE!

THE SAME WORD
"FILBERT"
JIM DAVIS 9-23

GARFIELD

ARE YOU READY, MY SON?
YES, MY FATHER
© 2000 PAWS, INC./Distributed by Universal Press Syndicate

FOR GENERATIONS OUR MEN HAVE BEEN TESTED

HE WHO CATCHES THE BRICK WILL LEAD OUR PEOPLE

I WILL MAKE YOU PROUD, MY FATHER
GOOD LUCK, MY SON

CLUNK

I GUESS THIS MEANS YOU'RE STILL THE LEADER
GO FIGURE
JIM DAVIS 9-24

OUT OF ORDER
JIM DAVIS 9-25

JON'S ALWAYS FOLLOWED HIS OWN FASHION PATH

SQUEEK
CLANK
SQUEEK
CLANK
SQUEEK
CLANK

STAINLESS STEEL TROUSERS
I AM SOOOO HIP
SQUEEK
CLANK
SQUEEK
JIM DAVIS 9-26

PHHHHHHHHHHHT!
JIM DAVIS 9-27

NOW YOU TRY IT

TOWEL, PLEASE

YOU'D BETTER NOT PICK ON ME, CAT, 'CAUSE IF YOU DO...
JIM DAVIS 9-28

I'LL TELL MY BIG BROTHER!

PLEASE SPARE ME
www.garfield.com

HEY, LADY, IT'S FRIDAY NIGHT!
JIM DAVIS 9-29

MAYBE YOU'D LIKE TO GO TO A MOVIE OR SOMETHING?

YOU CAN KNIT ANYTIME, GRANDMA!
A NEW REJECTION RECORD!
www.garfield.com

SOMETIMES I DON'T FEEL WANTED
JIM DAVIS 9-30

OH, GOODY, MAIL! ANYTHING FOR ME?
NOT MUCH...

JUST THIS EVICTION NOTICE FROM THE PLANET EARTH
www.garfield.com

GARFIELD

HEY! THERE'S CAT HAIR ALL OVER THE WAFFLE IRON!

TELL ME SOMETHING I DON'T KNOW!
JIM DAVIS 10-1

TAKING CARE OF A CAT ISN'T EASY, BUT IT'S WORTH IT!

TO THE CAT, I MEAN

HERE'S ANOTHER BALL OF YARN!

TWICE THE FUN

AH, THE SIMPLE PLEASURE OF LYING IN A BASKET OF FRESHLY WASHED LAUNDRY

GET OUT OF THERE

BE CAREFUL, LEST YOU OFFEND ZARTOK, EARTHLING!

I WAS PAINTING. YOU WERE SHEDDING
I LOVE WHAT YOU'VE DONE WITH THIS ROOM!

I THINK I'LL CHASE MY TAIL

GOTCHA

I DON'T KNOW WHAT DOGS SEE IN THIS
JIM DAVIS 10-6

LISTEN TO THAT!
RRRR
RRRR
RRRR

THERE'S NO MISTAKING THE PURRING OF A CONTENTED CAT
RRR
RRR
RRR

YOU FORGOT TO JIGGLE THE HANDLE AGAIN
RRR
RRR
JIM DAVIS 10-7

GARFIELD

BLAH BLAH BLAH BLAH BLAH...

BLAH BLAH BLAH BLAH BLAH...

BLAH BLAH BLAH BLAH BLAH...

BLAH BLAH BLAH BLAH BLAH...

BLAH BLAH BLAH BLAH BLAH...
JIM DAVIS 10-8

...AND ON DAYS WE DIDN'T HAVE CHORES
TO DO, DOC BOY AND I WOULD BORROW
THE TRACTOR AND DRIVE DOWN TO TOWN
WHERE THE REAL ACTION   'D HANG
OUT AT THE GAS STATION   TWO
BOTTLES OF POP AND O'   M WITH
OUR TEETH. THEN, DOC   COUNT
HOW MANY RED CARS DR   AND I'D
COUNT HOW   NY BLUE   OVE PAST

I COULD HAVE DONE THINGS WITH MY LIFE

BUT I DIDN'T

JIM DAVIS 10-9

SOMETIMES IT'S HARD TO EXPRESS OUR INNER FEELINGS
NONSENSE

I LOVE BACON!

YOUR TURN
JIM DAVIS 10-10

I'M GROWING A MOUSTACHE, GARFIELD

FACIAL HAIR IS MACHO, YOU KNOW

I'VE ALWAYS THOUGHT SO
JIM DAVIS 10-11

ODIE, YOU'RE SUCH A GOOD BOY!
JIM DAVIS 10-12

AND GARFIELD, YOU'RE SUCH A...SUCH A...

CAT
A "GOOD BOY" WOULD KILL YOU, WOULDN'T IT?
www.garfield.com

THAT BULLY DIDN'T LIKE ME LOOKING AT HIS GIRLFRIEND
JIM DAVIS 10-13

BUT THE JOKE'S ON HIM

MY TIE WAS DARN TASTY
THAT WILL TEACH HIM
www.garfield.com

JON AND ODIE AREN'T HOME
GARFIELD

I HATE BEING BY MYSELF
GARFIELD

THERE'S NO THRILL IN STEALING YOUR OWN FOOD
GARFIELD
JIM DAVIS 10-14

Garfield

Z

Z

Z

Z

Z

WHERE HAVE YOU BEEN?
TAKING A PROGRESSIVE NAP
JIM DAVIS 10-15

TAILS!
HEADS!
JIM DAVIS 10-16

HEADS!

WELCOME TO "CATNIP CORNER"!
www.garfield.com

TONIGHT, ON "WEIRD BUT TRUE," WE'RE INTERVIEWING A MAN WITH A RAILROAD SPIKE THROUGH HIS HEAD!
HI, BOB, GLAD TO BE HERE
www.garfield.com
JIM DAVIS 10-17

SO, SIR, HOW EXACTLY DID THIS HAPPEN?
HI, BOB, GLAD TO BE HERE

UH...HAS THIS AFFECTED YOU IN ANY WAY?
ASK HIM IF HE'S GLAD TO BE THERE!
HI, BOB, GLAD TO BE HERE

IT'S THE "BINKY THE CLOWN SHOW"!
www.garfield.com
JIM DAVIS 10-18

TODAY IS "HEALTH DAY," KIDS! LET'S SEE WHO'S AT THE DOOR...

WHY, IT'S "PETEY" THE BLOATED TICK!
THAT IS ONE UGLY PUPPET

OKAY, I ADMIT IT. I WAS WRONG. WHADDYA WANT, AN APOLOGY?!
ALL RIGHT, FINE! I'M SORRY, DO YOU HEAR ME?!...SORRY!
S-O-R-R-Y!!!
THE WEATHERMAN IS LOSING IT
JIM DAVIS 10-19
© 2000 PAWS, INC./Distributed by Universal Press Syndicate
www.garfield.com

I DID SOMETHING UNUSUAL LAST NIGHT, GARFIELD
© 2000 PAWS, INC./Distributed by Universal Press Syndicate

I VIDEOTAPED MY ENTIRE DATE!
CLICK
JIM DAVIS 10-20

HERE SHE IS SLASHING MY TIRES
SHE'S WAVING
www.garfield.com

WELCOME TO SIXTY MINUTES OF TELEVISED SILENCE
JIM DAVIS 10-21
www.garfield.com

READ A BOOK, WHY DON'T YOU?
QUALITY PROGRAMMING
© 2000 PAWS, INC./Distributed by Universal Press Syndicate

GARFIELD

MY HAIR'S ON FIRE!

ANKLE-BITING WOODCHUCKS!

I'M BEING DEPORTED TO MONGOLIA!

LOCUSTS!

YOUR DINNER WILL BE A TEENSE LATE

WHY DOES EVERYTHING HAPPEN TO ME?!
JIM DAVIS 10-22

NOW TAKE THAT GLASS OF MILK...

IS IT HALF FULL OR HALF EMPTY?
DEPENDS

DO YOU HAVE HALF A COOKIE?
JIM DAVIS 10-23

CLUCK CLUCK

CLUCK CLUCK

THAT MIGHT EXPLAIN THE FRIED HAT FOR DINNER
JIM DAVIS 10-24

DO NOT KICK THE DOG
JIM DAVIS 10-25

DO NOT KICK THE DOG

WHAP!

I FEEL KINDA LOW, MOM
JIM DAVIS 10-26

I HAVE NO FRIENDS, I CAN'T GET A DATE...

AND THE CAT IS WEARING MY UNDERWEAR
I PREFER YOUR BOXERS

I HAVE A DATE WITH SALLY TONIGHT, GARFIELD

SHE LIKES HER MEN STRONG AND RUGGED

I'M WEARING A GORILLA SUIT
WITH THOSE SHOES?
JIM DAVIS 10-27

MY MEMORIES... BY JON ARBUCKLE
JIM DAVIS 10-28

I WAS BORN ON A FARM

AND THEN I WROTE ABOUT MY BORING, EMPTY EXISTENCE
SHORT BUT HONEST

GARFIELD

I'M SORRY, SIR, YOU'RE TOO LATE. WE'RE NO LONGER SERVING BREAKFAST THIS MORNING
© 2000 PAWS, INC./Distributed by Universal Press Syndicate

SQUEEEZE

BOY, THAT SMARTS
JIM DAVIS 10-29

DING-DONG

DO YOU OWN AN ORANGE CAT?
UH, YES

MR. THROTTLE'S TULIP BED IS OFF LIMITS
LET'S SEE YOU SCRATCH YOUR NOSE

GARFIELD, I THINK WE HAVE VAMPIRES

THERE ARE TWO PUNCTURE HOLES IN MY DONUT

AND ALL THE JELLY'S BEEN SUCKED OUT!
I'LL BE IN MY COFFIN

DING-DONG

THE GUY IS HERE TO FIX THE ROOF

DING-DONG
JPM DAVPS 11-2

www.garfield.com

CAN WE SPARE A CUP OF ANTS?
© 2000 PAWS, INC./Distributed by Universal Press Syndicate

DING-DONG
JPM DAVPS 11-3

www.garfield.com

DO YOU WANT YOUR CAR WASHED?
© 2000 PAWS, INC./Distributed by Universal Press Syndicate

DING-DONG
JPM DAVPS 11-4

www.garfield.com

WHO WAS IT?
I NEVER DISCUSS EXISTENTIALISM BEFORE NOON
© 2000 PAWS, INC./Distributed by Universal Press Syndicate

GARFIELD

WHAT A BEAUTIFUL DAY!
© 2000 PAWS, INC./Distributed by Universal Press Syndicate

JIM DAVIS 11-5

ONLY ONE LITTLE CLOUD

...ONE STINKING LITTLE CLOUD

IT'S ALMOST TIME TO EAT

WHAT THINK, GARFIELD?
I'M GOING TO SAY THIS ONCE, JON

ANYTIME I'M NOT EATING IS "ALMOST TIME TO EAT"
JIM DAVIS 11-6

HEY, ODIE!

JIM DAVIS 11-7

NEVER MIND

I WONDER WHERE JON IS?

THE TOES ON MY RIGHT FOOT ARE HAIRIER THAN THE TOES ON MY LEFT FOOT!

LET'S PRETEND I COULDN'T FIND HIM
JIM DAVIS 11-8

DO YOU THINK YOU GET ENOUGH EXERCISE?
EXERCISE?

DO I GET ENOUGH EXERCISE?!

I THINK I JUST PULLED A MUSCLE
JIM DAVIS 11-9

JIM DAVIS 11-10

CLANG! CLANG! CLANG! CLANG! CLANG!

WHY DID YOU DO THAT?!
BECAUSE YOUR DATE IS AT THE DOOR

I MADE A LIST OF THE THINGS WE NEED FROM THE GROCERY...

"EVERYTHING"
GET TWO. I'M HUNGRY!
JIM DAVIS 11-11

GARF
IELD.

BZZZZZZZZZZL

ZZZZZZ

ZZZZZ

GOTCHA!
GRAB.
ZIP

HEY...

ARE YOU GONNA
EAT THAT?...
JIM DAVIS 11-12

IF YOU SQUISH ME, YOU'LL HATE YOURSELF IN THE MORNING!

NOT LIKELY

I'M NEVER UP BEFORE NOON
JIM DAVIS 11-13

YOU SQUISHED MY MOTHER! YOU SQUISHED MY FATHER!

YOU SQUISHED MY BROTHER! YOU SQUISHED MY SISTER! YOU SQUISHED MY SISTER! YOU SQUISHED MY SISTER! YOU SQUISHED MY BROTHER! YOU SQUISHED MY SISTER!

YOU SQUISHED MY BROTHER! YOU SQUISHED MY BROTHER! YOU SQUISHED MY SISTER!
LET'S HOPE HE'S THE LAST OF THE LINE
JIM DAVIS 11-14

OH, GREAT...MY HANDS ARE ASLEEP AND MY NOSE ITCHES!

A-HEM

HOWZAT?
SA' RIGHT
JIM DAVIS 11-15

HEY, CAT, THIS IS MY COUSIN, LOUIE THE TARANTULA

SMACK!

WHO, BY THE WAY, I NEVER REALLY LIKED
JIM DAVIS 11-16
www.garfield.com

I HAD A MOTH FOR DINNER LAST NIGHT

WAS IT GOOD?
YOU BET!
JIM DAVIS 11-17

FLAME BROILED TO PERFECTION ON THE PORCH LIGHT...NUM!
www.garfield.com

I FEEL LIKE TAKING ON THE WORLD!

?
www.garfield.com

JIM DAVIS 11-18

-G-A-R-F-I-E-L-D

RRRRR RRRRR

RRRRRR RRRRR

RRRRR RRRRR

RRRRRR RRRRR

OKAY, GARFIELD...
I LEFT YOU A SPOT

WHATTA GUY

THIS IS INTERESTING...
JIM DAVIS 11-20

SAYS HERE YOUR PET'S NAME SHOULD REFLECT ITS PERSONALITY
© 2000 PAWS, INC./Distributed by Universal Press Syndicate

WHAT THINK, SLOTH BOY?
COULD BE, THIMBLE BRAIN
www.garfield.com

I'M BORED

YOU'RE ALSO BORING
© 2000 PAWS, INC./Distributed by Universal Press Syndicate

YOU DO IT ALL!
www.garfield.com
JIM DAVIS 11-21

NO, THAT'S NOT IT
JIM DAVIS 11-22

IT WAS A STICK!
© 2000 PAWS, INC./Distributed by Universal Press Syndicate

I HATE FETCH
www.garfield.com

HI, I'M HOWIE THE HAPPY TURKEY!

BRRRR...I'M COLD! WOULD YOU PUT ME IN THE OVEN?

STOP IT, GARFIELD
I WANNA BE A SANDWICH!
JIM DAVIS 11-23

ELLEN, THIS IS JON
JIM DAVIS 11-24

CLICK

OH, NO! SOMEONE CUT HER PHONE LINE!
SOUNDS LIKE A JOB FOR DENIAL MAN

I REMEMBER THE MISCHIEF WE GOT INTO AS KIDS
JIM DAVIS 11-25

WE'D SNEAK UP TO A HOUSE...

AND FLIP THEIR WELCOME MAT OVER!
AH, THAT WOULD EXPLAIN YOUR KEY COLLECTION

GARFIELD

HMMM...FORGOT THE CATSUP

CLICK
WOOP *WOOP*

I SENSE A LACK OF TRUST HERE
STEP AWAY FROM THE MEAT LOAF!
JIM DAVIS 11-26

THE CHICKS, THEY JUST AREN'T DIGGING ME, GARFIELD. I GOTTA DO SOMETHING
© 2000 PAWS, INC. All Rights Reserved.

WELL, JON, PERHAPS YOU SHOULD STRIVE TO BECOME MORE EMPATHETIC TO THE FEMALE PSYCHE

THAT WOULD ENABLE YOU TO ESTABLISH A MORE MEANINGFUL DIALOG, THUS CONTRIBUTING TO DEEPER, MORE REWARDING RELATIONSHIPS
MAYBE A MANICURE
www.garfield.com
Distributed by Universal Press Syndicate
JIM DAVIS 11-27

SEE THAT GIRL STARING AT ME, GARFIELD?
Distributed by Universal Press Syndicate
JIM DAVIS 11-28

SHE CAN'T HELP IT

I'M A CHICK MAGNET
AN ABSENT-MINDED CHICK MAGNET
www.garfield.com
© 2000 PAWS, INC. All Rights Reserved.

MARSHA, I'M LOOKING FOR AN OLD-FASHIONED GIRL
JIM DAVIS 11-29

A GIRL WITH SOLID FAMILY VALUES...
Distributed by Universal Press Syndicate

A GIRL WHO CAN MILK A GOAT DRY IN THREE MINUTES FLAT!
BYE-BYE, MARSHA
www.garfield.com
© 2000 PAWS, INC. All Rights Reserved.

YESIREE, GARFIELD, THERE ARE A LOT OF WOMEN OUT THERE

YESIREE... PLENTY OF FISH IN THE SEA

I'LL JUST CAST OUT THE OLD LINE
YOUR BAIT'S DEAD
www.garfield.com
© 2000 PAWS, INC. All Rights Reserved.

HELLO, GRANDMA? THIS IS JON
Distributed by Universal Press Syndicate

WELL, I'M A LITTLE SAD. I CAN'T SEEM TO GET A DATE

SHE SAYS THAT'S BECAUSE I'M A DORK
I'M SURE SHE MEANT IT IN THE BEST POSSIBLE WAY
© 2000 PAWS, INC. All Rights Reserved.
www.garfield.com

YOU DON'T REMEMBER ME, BECKY?
Distributed by Universal Press Syndicate

NO?
ALL RIGHT!

REALLY?
ASK HER OUT!
JIM DAVIS 12-2
© 2000 PAWS, INC. All Rights Reserved.
www.garfield.com

Garfield

WELL, GARFIELD...

THE HOLIDAYS ARE COMING UP...

AND IT'S QUIET HERE...

TOO QUIET...

WAAAY TOO QUIET...
JIM DAVIS 12-3

MAYBE I SHOULD SING...
HARRUMPH
MEOW!
MEOW! MEOW!
SLAP
SLAP
SLAP
SLAP
BAM
BAM
BAM
BAM

I WONDER IF GARFIELD KNOWS CHRISTMAS IS COMING SOON

HUG

HE KNOWS
JIM DAVIS 12-4

SNOW ALWAYS MAKES IT FEEL MORE CHRISTMASY...

WELL, FAH LAH LAH LAH LAH...

WHAT IS THAT SNOWMAN DOING IN THE LIVING ROOM?

MELTING
JIM DAVIS 12-6

JON'S DECORATING THE CHRISTMAS TREE
JIM DAVIS 12-7

ZZT

FRAYED EXTENSION CORD
THAT AIN'T ALL THAT'S FRAYED, PAL
www.garfield.com

JIM DAVIS 12-8

SMACK!

GOT A NIFTY TREE TOPPER
GO AWAY!
www.garfield.com

JUST REMEMBER: SANTA IS WATCHING YOU
JIM DAVIS 12-9

HERE'S TO YOU, BIG GUY!
www.garfield.com

Garfield

WHUMP!

WHUMP!

?

WHUMP!

JUST
TESTING
JIM DAVIS 12-10

NEEDS
MORE LARD

I REMEMBER CHRISTMASES WHEN I WAS GROWING UP...
Distributed by Universal Press Syndicate
© 2000 PAWS, INC. All Rights Reserved.

...DAD CARVING THE ROAST FLY...

...THE YULE GNAT BURNING IN THE FIREPLACE...
YOU'RE PUTTING ME OFF MY EGGNOG HERE
JIM DAVIS 12-11
www.garfield.com

I REMEMBER BACK ON THE FARM, WE HAD AN ELECTRIC TOY TRAIN THAT RAN AROUND THE CHRISTMAS TREE
© 2000 PAWS, INC. All Rights Reserved.

THEN ONE YEAR DOC BOY LICKED THE TRACK
www.garfield.com

HE GLOWED FOR THREE DAYS
I TAKE BACK EVERYTHING I'VE SAID ABOUT HIM NOT BEING VERY BRIGHT
Distributed by Universal Press Syndicate
JIM DAVIS 12-12

BEHOLD: THE CANDY CANE...
© 2000 PAWS, INC. All Rights Reserved.

A HOLIDAY ICON...SLEEK... DAZZLING IN ITS SIMPLICITY
Distributed by Universal Press Syndicate

AND TOO DARN TASTY TO PONTIFICATE ON ANY LONGER
JIM DAVIS 12-13
www.garfield.com

HAAAAAHHHH
MMMMM

CANDY CANE BREATH
JIM DAVIS 12-14

LET'S MAKE A DEAL...
JIM DAVIS 12-15

YOU TELL ME WHERE YOU'VE HIDDEN MY CHRISTMAS PRESENT...

AND I WON'T RIP YOUR LIPS OFF AND THROW THEM ON THE ROOF
I DON'T LIKE THAT LOOK

...SO WHAT WOULD YOU SAY TO SANTA IF HE LOOKED YOU STRAIGHT IN THE EYE AND ASKED, "HAVE YOU BEEN **GOOD** THIS YEAR?"

PURRRRRRRRRRRRRRRR

THAT'S A KITTY CAT COP-OUT
SO WHAT? I'M DESPERATE
JIM DAVIS 12-16

Garfield

I CAN'T TAKE MUCH MORE OF THIS...

THE WAITING...

THE NOT KNOWING...

HOW IS ANYONE SUPPOSED TO STAND THIS KIND OF SUSPENSE

FOR...FOR...
JIM DAVIS 12-17

EIGHT MORE DAYS
EIGHT MORE DAYS?!!

SLAM!

IT WAS HORRIBLE! I BARELY ESCAPED WITH MY LIFE!!

CHRISTMAS SHOPPING AT THE MALL
JIM DAVIS 12-18

GARFIELD!
JIM DAVIS 12-19

THAT WAS THE SHOPPING MALL CALLING!

SANTA'S ELF WANTS HIS BOOTIES BACK
THE CRYBABY

LOOK WHAT CAME, GARFIELD... A CHRISTMAS PACKAGE FROM MY MOM!

OKAY, I'M GOING TO CUT THE STRING...
CAREFUL... DON'T SPILL THE GRAVY
JIM DAVIS 12-20

HAVE YOU BEEN CLIMBING THE CHRISTMAS TREE?
JIM DAVIS 12-21

NOT OURS
© 2000 PAWS, INC. All Rights Reserved.
Distributed by Universal Press Syndicate
www.garfield.com

COVER FOR ME
DING DONG

SIGH...WHAT GREAT CHRISTMAS MEMORIES...
PHOTOS

BUT, YOU KNOW, WE SHOULDN'T LIVE IN THE PAST...
I CERTAINLY DON'T
PHOTOS
© 2000 PAWS, INC. All Rights Reserved.
www.garfield.com
Distributed by Universal Press Syndicate

I LIVE FOR THE PRESENT!
GARFIELD
JIM DAVIS 12-22

I'M VERY SORRY, MRS. FEENY. HAPPY HOLIDAYS TO YOU TOO

SHE SAYS YOU LEFT A PRESENT ON HER DOORMAT
'TIS THE SEASON FOR GIVING
© 2000 PAWS, INC. All Rights Reserved.
www.garfield.com
Distributed by Universal Press Syndicate

A HAIRBALL?!!
I MADE IT MYSELF
JIM DAVIS 12-25

GARFIELD
© 2000 PAWS, INC. All Rights Reserved.
JIM DAVIS 12-24
PANT
PANT
PANT
PANT
PANT
PANT
SQUEAK
SQUEAK
SQUEAK
Distributed by Universal Press Syndicate

I LOVE CHRISTMAS
SO DO I
AND I LOVE YOU, GARFIELD
SO DO I
www.garfield.com
© 2000 PAWS, INC. All Rights Reserved. Distributed by Universal Press Syndicate
JIM DAVIS 12-25
AND WE ALL LOVE YOU!
MERRY CHRISTMAS!

SO LONG, CHRISTMAS! GOOD-BYE!
Distributed by Universal Press Syndicate

DON'T BE A STRANGER!
www.garfield.com
© 2000 PAWS, INC. All Rights Reserved.
JIM DAVIS 12-26

HI, DENISE, IT'S JON! ARE YOU DOING ANYTHING FOR NEW YEARS?
Distributed by Universal Press Syndicate
JIM DAVIS 12-27

© 2000 PAWS, INC. All Rights Reserved.
www.garfield.com

I MEAN BESIDES AVOIDING ME AT ALL COSTS
ZING!

NOBODY WILL GO OUT WITH ME ON NEW YEAR'S
Distributed by Universal Press Syndicate

DON'T FEEL BAD, JON

THEY WOULDN'T GO OUT WITH YOU EVEN IF IT WEREN'T NEW YEAR'S
PAT PAT
PAT PAT
JIM DAVIS 12-28
© 2000 PAWS, INC. All Rights Reserved.
www.garfield.com

WHY CAN'T I GET A DATE?!
JIM DAVIS 12-29

WHAT AM I? UGLY?...NO!
WHAT AM I? IMPOLITE?...NO!
WHAT AM I? BORING?...
Distributed by Universal Press Syndicate

Z
OH, SHUT UP!
© 2000 PAWS, INC. All Rights Reserved.
www.garfield.com

DATING IS OVERRATED
Distributed by Universal Press Syndicate

NEW YEAR'S IS OVERRATED

DATES ON NEW YEAR'S, HOWEVER, ARE NOT
WAAAH!
JIM DAVIS 12-30
© 2000 PAWS, INC. All Rights Reserved.
www.garfield.com

GARFIELD

31 1

HERE'S YOUR MAIL

AND HERE'S THE MAILMAN'S WALLET

LEAVE THE POOR MAN ALONE!
BOY, ARE HIS KIDS UGLY
JIM DAVIS 1-1

WHAT DO YOU WANT TO DO?

OKAY

JIM DAVIS 1-2

HOME IS WHERE YOU CAN WALK AROUND IN YOUR UNDERWEAR
JIM DAVIS 1-3

HOME IS WHERE YOU CAN DRINK MILK OUT OF THE CARTON

HOME IS WHERE YOU CAN SCRATCH WHERE IT ITCHES
HOME IS DISGUSTING

I MET A REPORTER YESTERDAY, GARFIELD

SHE WAS LOOKING FOR A HUMAN-INTEREST STORY

SHE TOOK MY PICTURE!
"PARK ATTRACTS GEEKS"
JIM DAVIS 1·4
© 2001 PAWS, INC. All Rights Reserved.
www.garfield.com

FRIDAY NIGHT...
Distributed by Universal Press Syndicate

AND I'M HOME WITH A CAT!
www.garfield.com

COULD ANYONE BE MORE DEPRESSED?
JIM DAVIS 1-5
© 2001 PAWS, INC. All Rights Reserved.

MY LIFE STINKS, GARFIELD... LIKE A WET DOG
JIM DAVIS 1-6
Distributed by Universal Press Syndicate

LIKE OLD SWEAT SOCKS...

LIKE...
I GET THE POINT!
© 2001 PAWS, INC. All Rights Reserved.
www.garfield.com

GARFIELD

DONK!
DONK?
DONK?
JIM DAVIS 1-7

DONK
DONK
DONK
DONK
DONK
WOW! LOOK AT THAT!

GOLF BALL-SIZED HAIL!
DONK
DONK
DONK
DONK

DONK
DONK
DONK
DONK
DONK

HE REALLY SHOULD SEEK PROFESSIONAL HELP
DONK
THWOCK

I DIDN'T BUY ANY KITTY TREATS, GARFIELD, AND DO YOU KNOW WHY?

BECAUSE LIFE IS NOT A TREAT, THAT'S WHY

REMEMBER THAT AS I PULL OUT A NECK HAIR
JIM DAVIS 1-8
© 2001 PAWS, INC. All Rights Reserved.
www.garfield.com

I HAVE THINGS TO DO!
Distributed by Universal Press Syndicate

I HAVE PLACES TO GO!

SO, THAT'S WHAT HAVING A LIFE FEELS LIKE
NEVER HURTS TO PRACTICE
JIM DAVIS 1-9
© 2001 PAWS, INC. All Rights Reserved.
www.garfield.com

TIME TO REFLECT ON THE DAY...
JIM DAVIS 1-10

YAAAAAAHHH!!
Distributed by Universal Press Syndicate

WHY DO YOU DO THAT TO YOURSELF?
© 2001 PAWS, INC. All Rights Reserved.
www.garfield.com

ODIE...A WATER BALLOON...
JiM DAViS 1-11

A CLAW...

THAT DIDN'T TURN OUT QUITE HOW I HAD HOPED

"THE CREW OF THE DOOMED SHIP HAD LOST HOPE"
JiM DAViS 1-12

"PROVISIONS GONE...NO ONE HAD EATEN IN DAYS..."

"THE SHIP'S CAT APPEARED ON DECK..."
BEDTIME!

WE HAD A CAT BACK ON THE FARM, GARFIELD
JiM DAViS 1-13

HE WAS A GREAT RATTER. THE BIGGER THE BETTER!

YOU WOULD HAVE LIKED HIM
I DON'T HANG WITH PSYCHOS

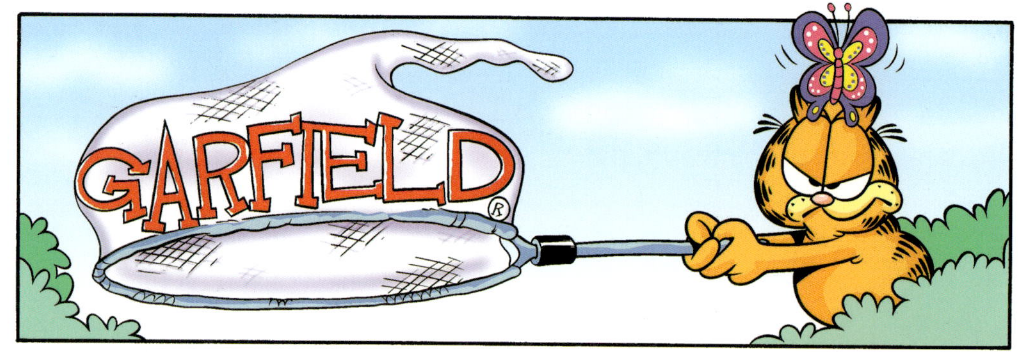

GARFIELD

YOU WILL GO OUT
WITH ME?!...IF I WHAT?...

CLUCK-CLUCK-
BUCK-BUC-BUC-
BUC-KAWW...

AM I
WHAT?

YES, I'M
FLAPPING
MY ARMS
HEAVEN FORBID
HE SHOULD
EMBARRASS
HIMSELF
IN FRONT OF
THE CAT

QUIET ON THE SET!
JIM DAVIS 1-15

ACTION!

NICE TRY

ALL IS RIGHT WITH MY UNIVERSE

STRINGMAAAAN!
JIM DAVIS 1-16

GOTTA GET A SMALLER UNIVERSE

I HAVE MANY HOPES AND DREAMS FOR THE FUTURE

I HAVE A SALAMI SANDWICH!

HOW ABOUT DREAMING UP SOME ICED TEA?
JIM DAVIS 1-17

BEEN EATING THOSE FRUIT-SHAPED REFRIGERATOR MAGNETS AGAIN?
MAYBE

BAT

BAT
BAT
BAT
BAT
BAT
BAT

MY PARENTS WANTED ME TO BE A SWEATER, BUT NOOOOOO...

EMPIRES RISE AND FALL
HISTORY

SEE?!
HISTORY

WHY RISE?!
HISTORY

GARFIELD® wuz heere

HELLO, IS EVELYN THERE?

WHAT'S THAT? SHE DOESN'T LIVE THERE ANYMORE?

SHE'S HOPPED A FREIGHTER FOR BORNEO?

SHE'S FORSWORN ALL HER MATERIAL POSSESSIONS AND MODERN WAYS OF LIVING?

WOW

SHE DIDN'T MENTION THAT ON OUR DATE LAST NIGHT
YOU DO HAVE THAT EFFECT ON WOMEN

TODAY WASN'T A GOOD DAY

BUT I GUESS IT WASN'T A BAD DAY EITHER

SO YOU'RE SAYING IT WASN'T A DAY AT ALL
JIM DAVIS 1-22

I'M NOT GOING TO SHED ANYMORE

I'VE CONTRACTED THE JOB OUT

JIM DAVIS 1-23

OUT THERE ARE ALL OF NATURE'S WONDERS!

IN HERE ARE CORN CHIPS AND DIP
JIM DAVIS 1-24

I WANT IT ALL!
DIP

CRIME, TAXES, WAR, STRIFE...
NEWS
CAT NEWS

NATURAL DISASTERS, ECONOMIC RUIN...
NEWS
CAT NEWS

SIGH...
THERE SURE IS A LOT OF SHEDDING IN THIS WORLD
NEWS
CAT NEWS
JIM DAVIS 1-25

MAKE A NOTE, GARFIELD

NEVER EAT A GOLDFISH RIGHT BEFORE BEDTIME
JIM DAVIS 1-26

YOU!

REMEMBER THIS!

IT'S NOT POLITE TO POINT!
JIM DAVIS 1-27

HERE'S EARL WITH THE EARLY-MORNING FARM REPORT
VAN, THERE'S NOTHING BUT DIRT AS FAR AS THE EYE CAN SEE
EARL, ANY TRACTOR SIGHTINGS?
CITY BOYS

WE'RE VISITING REX THE STUNT DOG
REX, WHAT DO YOU GET PAID FOR ALL THOSE DANGEROUS STUNTS?
WELL, THEY PAT ME ON THE HEAD A LOT
THE DUMB WORK CHEAP

THE REMOTE IS BROKEN
CLICK CLICK
AND I'M WATCHING "THE HISTORY OF NORWEGIAN FLOWERPOTS"
LETHARGY CERTAINLY EXPANDS YOUR HORIZONS

GARFIELD

EVERY ANIMAL HAS A SPECIAL PLACE...

WE CATS FAVOR WINDOWSILLS
Distributed by Universal Press Syndicate

THE LUXURY OF LYING IN THE WARM SUNLIGHT...

THE PANORAMIC VIEW OF THE WORLD...THE PASSING PARADE OF HUMANITY
© 2001 PAWS, INC. All Rights Reserved.

WE CATS FAVOR THE FLOOR...
JIM DAVIS 2-4

HELLO, MOM
JIM DAVIS 2-5

OH, THE SAME OLD THING

RIGHT NOW I'M DUSTING THE CAT
HEE HEE HEE
© 2001 PAWS, INC. All Rights Reserved.

GARFIELD, I HEAR SOMETHING IN THE BASEMENT!
JIM DAVIS 2-6

IT COULD BE A HUGE RAT!

DOESN'T THAT INFLAME YOUR PRIMAL INSTINCTS?
YES, I'LL BE IN THE CAR
© 2001 PAWS, INC. All Rights Reserved.

RESERVED

RESERVED

IS IT POSSIBLE THAT I'VE LOST THE ELEMENT OF SURPRISE?
JIM DAVIS 2-7
© 2001 PAWS, INC. All Rights Reserved.

ODIE DUG UP THE FLOWERS IN THE GARDEN!
www.garfield.com
Distributed by Universal Press Syndicate

OOPS
JIM DAVIS 2-8

ODIE DUG UP THE FLOWERS IN THE GARDEN!
© 2001 PAWS, INC. All Rights Reserved.

CONGRATULATIONS, YOU HAVE WON THE GRAND PRIZE!
Distributed by Universal Press Syndicate
www.garfield.com

AN EVENING WITH ME

THE EXCITEMENT WAS TOO MUCH
PROBABLY A STOMACH VIRUS
JIM DAVIS 2-9
© 2001 PAWS, INC. All Rights Reserved.

NOBODY CAN STRETCH LIKE A CAT
JIM DAVIS 2-10
Distributed by Universal Press Syndicate
www.garfield.com

YAWN

HEY!
© 2001 PAWS, INC. All Rights Reserved.

GARFIELD

I'M PRETTY MUCH SICK OF WINTER
Distributed by Universal Press Syndicate

ENOUGH WITH THE SNOW ALREADY!

© 2001 PAWS, INC. All Rights Reserved.

JIM DAVIS 2-11

ZIP

I HAVE A SIMPLE PHILOSOPHY, GARFIELD
JIM DAViS 2-12
Distributed by Universal Press Syndicate
www.garfield.com

LAUGH, AND THE WORLD LAUGHS WITH YOU

IN FACT, I CAN HEAR THEM NOW
THEY CAMP ON THE LAWN
© 2001 PAWS, INC. All Rights Reserved.

POOF!
Cookies
Distributed by Universal Press Syndicate
www.garfield.com

I AM THE GENIE OF THE COOKIE JAR!
Cookies
JIM DAViS 2-13

YOU HAVE THREE WISHES!
WHERE'S A COOKIE WHEN YOU NEED ONE?
© 2001 PAWS, INC. All Rights Reserved.

I'M NOT DOING ANYTHING TODAY, GARFIELD
ATTA BOY
Distributed by Universal Press Syndicate
www.garfield.com

I'M BEING LAZY
MY HERO

I'M NOT EVEN CHANGING YOUR LITTER BOX
PSYCHO!
JIM DAViS 2-14
© 2001 PAWS, INC. All Rights Reserved.

JON, LET'S SAVOR THIS MOMENT
I HAVE A BANANA IN MY EAR
JIM DAVIS 2-15

SOMEDAY WE'LL REMEMBER WHEN YOU TRIPPED OVER ME COMING BACK FROM THE GROCERY...AND LAUGH!
THERE ARE GRAPES UP MY NOSE

THESE ARE THE GOOD OLD DAYS!
I'M GOING TO KILL YOU

ENJOY YOUR DINNER, GARFIELD?
VERY TASTY

I CALL IT "BACK-OF-THE-FRIDGE-BOTTOM-SHELF-BEHIND-THE-BAKING-SODA STEW"

I CAN ONLY MAKE IT ABOUT ONCE EVERY FIVE YEARS
THAT'S JUST A LITTLE BIT MORE THAN I NEEDED TO KNOW
JIM DAVIS 2-16

I'M BORED, TIRED AND HUNGRY

YEAH, BUT CAN YOU SHED? HUH? HUH?!
JIM DAVIS 2-17

GARFIELD

POOKY! YOU'RE WARM!
YOU'VE BEEN HUGGED
RECENTLY, AND NOT
BY ME!

HAVE YOU BEEN
HUGGING AROUND?!

I JUST GOT
YOUR BEAR OUT
OF THE DRYER

I'M SUCH A
JEALOUS FOOL!
JIM DAVIS 2-18

CHICKS DIG THE TOUGH-GUY LOOK

SO I GOT THIS LEATHER JACKET. WHAT THINK, GARFIELD?

IT GOES WELL WITH YOUR BUNNY SLIPPERS

I'M NOT YOUR TYPE?!

WELL JUST WHAT IS YOUR TYPE?

HUMAN?
PICKY, PICKY, PICKY

CINDY JUST CALLED

PLPLPLPLPLPL!!

SHE SAID I WAS IMMATURE
WHAT DOES SHE KNOW?

WOULD YOU REPEAT THAT?
JIM DAVIS 2-22
www.garfield.com
Distributed by Universal Press Syndicate

YOU WILL GO OUT WITH ME?!

HELLO?... HELLO?
JON WILL BE RIGHT BACK. HE'S IN THE FRONT YARD DOING HIS HAPPY CHICKEN DANCE
YES! YES! OH, YES!
© 2001 PAWS, INC. All Rights Reserved.

I HAVE A DATE WITH GINNY TONIGHT
www.garfield.com
Distributed by Universal Press Syndicate

SHE LOVES TO LAUGH

I HAVE THREE HOURS TO GET A SENSE OF HUMOR
I'LL GET THE FAKE FOREHEAD FAUCET
JIM DAVIS 2-23
© 2001 PAWS, INC. All Rights Reserved.

SOME KIDS HAVE BEEN RINGING OUR DOORBELL AND RUNNING
www.garfield.com
Distributed by Universal Press Syndicate

THIS BUCKET OF WATER WILL TEACH THEM A LESSON!
DING DONG

MY DATE WILL BE HERE ANY SECOND
I DON'T THINK SO
JIM DAVIS 2-24
© 2001 PAWS, INC. All Rights Reserved.

Garfield

OOOOOOOOG...

GURGLE
ARGLE
ARGLE

NOOGLE
ARGLE
GARGLE
OOGLE

ARGULEY
OOOGLEY
RARG-A-
RARG-
ROOG-
OOG-
OOG
A-CHOOB

IT HAS A NICE MELODY, BUT YOU CAN'T DANCE TO IT

HUNGRY CATS HAVE NO SENSE OF HUMOR

THERE ARE TWO REASONS WHY I HATE SPIDERS
JIM DAVIS 2-26

THEY'RE SNEAKY...
SPLAT!

AND I SUSPECT THEY'RE STEALING FOOD
CLANK
DONK

I'M THE AVENGING SPIDER!
JIM DAVIS 2-27

KICK

I STRIKE AGAIN!
SCRATCH SCRATCH

JIM DAVIS 2-28
GO AWAY

AHA! IS IT MY VIOLENT NATURE AND RUTHLESS HERITAGE THAT THREATENS YOU?...

OR IS IT MY IMPOSING, HAIRY BODY AND LONG VENOMOUS FANGS?
IT'S YOUR FLY BREATH. NOW GO AWAY

JIM DAVIS 3-1
SMACK!

© 2001 PAWS, INC. All Rights Reserved.
YOU'RE LATE!
SORRY

JIM DAVIS 3-2
I DON'T HAVE TIME TO STOP!
www.garfield.com
Distributed by Universal Press Syndicate

SMACK!

© 2001 PAWS, INC. All Rights Reserved.
YOU MUST LEARN TO RELAX
HOW'S THIS?

SPIDER!
WAIT!
JIM DAVIS 3-3

SPIDERS EAT INSECTS!
www.garfield.com
Distributed by Universal Press Syndicate

© 2001 PAWS, INC. All Rights Reserved.
INSECT EATER!
SMACK!

Garfield

WHACK!

?

WHEEEEEEEE!!
BLAT!
JIM DAVIS 3-4

SLORP!
SLURP!
SLUP!
SLURP!

PLEASE, GARFIELD, THERE'S NOTHING MORE DISGUSTING THAN THAT!
SLORP!
SLUP!

EXCEPT THAT
© 2001 PAWS, INC. All Rights Reserved.
JIM DAVIS 3-5

GARFIELD, HELP! I LOCKED MYSELF OUT GETTING THE PAPER!
JIM DAVIS 3-6

HURRY! I DON'T HAVE ANY PANTS ON!

I'M WEARING THE PUPPY UNDERWEAR!
THEN COME IN THROUGH THE PET DOOR
© 2001 PAWS, INC. All Rights Reserved.

JIM DAVIS 3-7

TOMORROW I'M GOING BACK TO GETTING DRESSED AFTER I TAKE MY SHOWER!
WELL, AT LEAST YOU TRIED SOMETHING
© 2001 PAWS, INC. All Rights Reserved.

RRRRRRrrrrrr

GARFIELD, WAS THAT THE BLENDER?

FORGET IT, I DON'T WANT TO KNOW
BUNNY-SLIPPER FRAPPÉ?
JIM DAVIS 3-8

I KNOW HOW TO GET A WOMAN'S ATTENTION
JIM DAVIS 3-9

WHO WANTS TO HEAR SOME BARNYARD IMITATIONS?!

WELL, THAT GOT HER ATTENTION
I DIDN'T KNOW ANYONE COULD RUN THAT FAST IN HEELS

HEH, HEH, HEH...
JIM DAVIS 3-10

OH, THE TROUBLE I COULD CAUSE!

IF MY CLAWS WEREN'T STUCK IN THE TABLE

MY COFFEE'S COLD

BOY, I HATE COLD COFFEE. HATE IT. HATE IT. HATE IT

NOPE, THERE'S NOTHING IN THE WORLD WORSE THAN COLD COFFEE
SLAP SLAP SLAP

I'LL BET IF I TRIED AS HARD AS I COULD, I COULDN'T POSSIBLY THINK OF ANYTHING WORSE THAN COLD COFFEE
TWITCH TWITCH

EEEEYAAAAAAHHH!!!
SKREENK

OKAY... SOGGY SHORTS,— MAYBE
JIM DAVIS 3-11

C'MON, GARFIELD...
UP AN' AT 'EM!

LIFE IS CALLING!

TELL LIFE TO LEAVE A MESSAGE

...IT'S NOT LIKE I HAVEN'T DONE ANYTHING WITH MY LIFE...

OH, WAIT A MINUTE...

YES, IT IS!

YOU APOLOGIZE TO ODIE FOR WHAT YOU DID TO HIM, OR I'LL PUNISH YOU SEVERELY!

PUNISH ME SEVERELY

WANNA HEAR ABOUT MY DAY?
JIM DAVIS 3-15

I'M NOT PAYING FOR THIS CARD!
NO

THERE ARE MANY, MANY THINGS I WILL NEVER UNDERSTAND
JIM DAVIS 3-16

AND THEY'RE ALL WOMEN
A RARE MOMENT OF HONESTY

THIS IS "NATIONAL UGLY FISH WEEK"

SO EAT AN UGLY FISH TODAY...

AND LEAVE THE PLANET THAT MUCH LESS UGLY
SLOGAN NEEDS WORK
JIM DAVIS 3-17

GARFIELD

© 2001 PAWS, INC. All Rights Reserved.

Distributed by Universal Press Syndicate

JIM DAVIS 3-18

ENJOY THE LITTLE THINGS,
AND THE BIG THINGS WILL TAKE
CARE OF THEMSELVES

MA, CAN I ASK YOU SOMETHING?
OF COURSE, TIMMY

CAN I HAVE A PET?
A PET?

HE FOLLOWED ME HOME, MA
YOU'RE NOT VERY BRIGHT, ARE YOU, TIMMY?
JIM DAVIS 3-19

JIM DAVIS 3-20

WATCH OUT FOR THE SPIDER!

SOME LOOKOUT YOU ARE
SORRY

YOU'D BETTER NOT MESS WITH ME! KNOW WHY?

SMACK!

BECAUSE YOU'RE SO TOUGH?
AND DON'T YOU FORGET IT
JIM DAVIS 3-21

...AND WITH A KISS FROM THE BEAUTIFUL PRINCESS...
SPIDER BEDTIME STORIES
JiM DAViS 3-22

THE FROG TURNED INTO A HANDSOME SPIDER...
SPIDER BEDTIME STORIES
www.garfield.com
Distributed by Universal Press Syndicate

WHICH THE PRINCESS STOMPED FLAT!
HEY! HEY! STICK TO THE STORY!
SPIDER BEDTIME STORIES
© 2001 PAWS, INC. All Rights Reserved.

HEY, CAT, I'M GONNA HOP ON YOUR NECK AND SUCK OUT ALL YOUR BODILY FLUIDS
www.garfield.com
Distributed by Universal Press Syndicate

Whack!

HEY! YOU CRIMPED MY STRAW!
JiM DAViS 3-23
© 2001 PAWS, INC. All Rights Reserved.

THIS IS MY COLLEGE INTERN
www.garfield.com
Distributed by Universal Press Syndicate

Smack!

HE DOES GOOD WORK
I THINK SO
JiM DAViS 3-24
© 2001 PAWS, INC. All Rights Reserved.

GARFIELD

I'LL BE SHAVING, IN CASE ANYONE CALLS FOR ME

Distributed by Universal Press Syndicate

BUZZZZZZZZZZZ
© 2001 PAWS, INC. All Rights Reserved.

BUZZZZZZZZZZZZZZZ

CLICK
JIM DAVIS 3-25

JUST CHECKING... DID ANYONE CALL?
THE PARANOIA POLICE SEND THEIR REGARDS

LIFE
STINKS

YOU SHOULD HAVE A MORE POSITIVE ATTITUDE

LIFE
STINKS
JIM DAVIS 3-26

I'M THINKING ABOUT WRITING THE STORY OF MY LIFE

MAYBE I SHOULD ACTUALLY DO SOMETHING FIRST
THAT WOULD REALLY HELP WITH THE TITLE
JIM DAVIS 3-27

REMEMBER THAT DAY AT THE AMUSEMENT PARK, GARFIELD?
HOW CAN I FORGET?
PHOTOS
JIM DAVIS 3-28

THEY SURE HAD SOME SCARY RIDES
EMBARRASSING...
PHOTOS

I COULDN'T STOP SCREAMING
BUT, IN THE PARKING LOT, JON?
PHOTOS

WHEN COMMUNICATING WITH PETS...
PETS
JIM DAVIS 3-29

KEEP COMMANDS SIMPLE AND TO THE POINT
PETS

LOSE... SOME... WEIGHT
GET... A... LIFE
PETS

MAYBE I'LL GET TOGETHER WITH FRIENDS TONIGHT

WE'LL LAUGH AND ENGAGE IN STIMULATING CONVERSATION...

OR MAYBE I'LL STAY HOME AND FLOSS
REALITY SETS IN
JIM DAVIS 3-30

DO YOU KNOW WHAT'S WRONG WITH CATS?

THEY...
CLICK

HEY!
YOU WATCH TOO MUCH TELEVISION
JIM DAVIS 3-31

GARFIELD
Z

WE SHOULD DO SOMETHING

HOW ABOUT MAILING MRS. FEENY'S LITTLE DOG TO AN OBSCURE OVERSEAS NATION WITH INSUFFICIENT POSTAGE?

OR WE COULD THUMB WRESTLE FOR THAT LAST PIECE OF CHEESECAKE

OR WE COULD HIJACK AN ICE CREAM TRUCK AND HOLD THE DRIVER HOSTAGE FOR THE WORLD'S LARGEST NUTTY-BUDDY

OR WE COULD PAINT OURSELVES PURPLE, SIT IN THE BATHTUB TOO LONG, AND PRETEND WE'RE RAISINS

CHECKERS?
I'M RED THIS TIME
JIM DAVIS 4-1

GARFIELD, THREE MICE JUST WALKED THROUGH THE FRONT DOOR

HAVEN'T YOU HEARD?

THEY WERE CARRYING SUITCASES!
THE CHEESE EXPO IS IN TOWN
JIM DAVIS 4-2

HMMM...WHAT SHOULD I DO ABOUT THIS NEW MOUSEHOLE?

OF COURSE!

ACCEPT A BRIBE!
JIM DAVIS 4-3

GARFIELD, THIS IS A DIAGRAM OF THE FOOD CHAIN
JIM DAVIS 4-4

YOU'RE HERE, AND THAT'S A MOUSE DOWN THERE...

ANY QUESTIONS?
WHERE'S PIZZA?

WOOF

UH... GARFIELD?...
YES, I KNOW. THEY'RE MAKING DOGS SMALLER THESE DAYS, AREN'T THEY?
JIM DAVIS 4-5

SNAP!
OUCH!
JIM DAVIS 4-6

SNAP!
OUCH!

SNAP!
OUCH!
HE'LL GIVE UP, EVENTUALLY
MAY I HAVE THE BAIT?

WE NEED A FOURTH FOR BRIDGE
JIM DAVIS 4-7

OKAY, BUT THIS TIME WE USE MY CARDS

LAST GAME I ABOUT WENT BLIND

Garfield

© 2001 PAWS, INC. All Rights Reserved.

Distributed by Universal Press Syndicate

JIM DAVIS 4-8

YOU'RE GOING TO HURT ME NOW, AREN'T YOU?
UNLESS YOU ACT POSTHASTE TO RECTIFY THIS UNFORTUNATE SITUATION

GARFIELD, IF YOU EXERCISED YOU'D HAVE MORE ENERGY
Distributed by Universal Press Syndicate
www.garfield.com

© 2001 PAWS, INC. All Rights Reserved.

AND THAT'S GOOD
AH
JIM DAVIS 4-9

AH, SPRINGTIME!
Distributed by Universal Press Syndicate
www.garfield.com

A TIME WHEN... UH...UM...
JIM DAVIS 4-10

WHAT DOES HAPPEN IN SPRINGTIME?
YOU HOLD YOUR ARM IN THE AIR?
© 2001 PAWS, INC. All Rights Reserved.

GARFIELD, YOU NEED TO DO SOME WORK
UH HUH
JIM DAVIS 4-11
Distributed by Universal Press Syndicate
www.garfield.com

YOU CAN HELP ME IN THE GARDEN
SURE

I MADE THIS LITTLE PLOW
YOU HAVE WAAAY TOO MUCH TIME ON YOUR HANDS
© 2001 PAWS, INC. All Rights Reserved.

HI, MOM...I MISS YOU TOO

YES, I REALIZE IT'S BEEN A LONG TIME SINCE I VISITED YOU...

YEEESSS, I REALIZE YOU'RE NOT GETTING ANY YOUNGER...
I'LL PACK MY FOOD BOWL AND TEDDY BEAR

I JUST LOVE CAR TRIPS...

THEY MAKE ME FEEL LIKE SINGING!

SLAM! SLAM!
BOYS?... BOYS?

MOM!
JONNY!

DAD!
SON!

JELLY BELLY!
LAME BRAIN!
BROTHERS

GOOD TO SEE YOU AGAIN, SON. YOU'RE LOOKING WELL
THANKS... YOU TOO, DAD
JIM DAVIS 4-19

WELL, GOT CHORES TO DO
BETTER GO UNPACK
(SNIFF) A REAL FATHER-SON MOMENT

GARFIELD ISN'T MUCH FOR THE FARM LIFE, IS HE, JONNY?
I GUESS NOT, MOM
JIM DAVIS 4-20

BUT HE'LL LEARN TO COPE
AAAGGHH!

ONLY THREE CHANNELS?!!

SEE THAT, GARFIELD? THOSE ARE SHEEP
LOOK LIKE DUST BUNNIES WITH LEGS

THAT'S WHERE WOOL COMES FROM
HOLD ON...

IF THIS IS ANYTHING LIKE THAT CHICKEN/EGG THING, I DON'T WANNA KNOW
JIM DAVIS 4-21

garfield

SURE IS A BEAUTIFUL SUNSET, DAD
Distributed by Universal Press Syndicate

YUP

SUNSETS ARE VERY POPULAR ON THE FARM...
JIM DAVIS 4-22

VERY POPULAR

WHAT ARE YOU?
I'M A ROOSTER

WHAT DO YOU DO?
I WAKE YOU UP AT THE CRACK OF DAWN

I DIDN'T HEAR THE ROOSTER THIS MORNING
I IMAGINE IT'S TOUGH TO CROW WITH BALING TWINE TIED AROUND ONE'S BEAK
JIM DAVIS 4-23

REMEMBER THAT TREE, JON? OUR BULL CHASED YOU UP THAT TREE
YEAH, DAD

BOY, YOU WERE STUCK UP THERE A LONG TIME...
I REMEMBER, DAD
JIM DAVIS 4-24

HOW OLD WERE YOU?
SEVEN AND EIGHT

SO HOW'S LIFE IN THE BIG CITY, JON?
JIM DAVIS 4-25

IT'S WILD!

SOMETIMES I STAY UP TILL TEN
MA!

FARMING CAN BE DANGEROUS, GARFIELD

THERE ARE WARNING SIGNS ALL OVER

"DO NOT TICKLE THE BULL"?
THAT'S A BIGGIE

I HAVE A GIRLFRIEND NOW, JON
REALLY?

WANT TO SEE A PICTURE OF HER?
SURE!

WHAT DO YOU THINK?
SAAAAY...
THAT'S ONE SHINY TOOTH

I'D LIKE TO STAY AND VISIT, JON, BUT I HAVE A DATE

LOOK AT THAT UGLY HOLSTEIN OVER THERE

THAT'S MY DATE
YOU SHOULDN'T WEAR POLKA DOTS, LADY!

Garfield

JIM DAVIS 4-29
SKITTER SKITTER

© 2001 PAWS, INC. All Rights Reserved.
* CLICK *
SCOUT TO BASE...

NO SIGN OF CAT...PROCEED

Distributed by Universal Press Syndicate

Whack!
Whack!
Whack!
Whack!

SCOUT TO BASE... UH, HOW'S YOUR SENSE OF HUMOR?

THIS ROOM WOULD LOOK BETTER WITH LESS CAT HAIR
JIM DAVIS 4-30

THERE'S NO CAT HAIR IN HERE EXCEPT WHAT'S ON ME

HEY!

THIS IS MRS. SPITTLE, MY THIRD-GRADE TEACHER
JIM DAVIS 5-1
YEAR BOOK

SHE HATED ME. SHE MADE ME TAKE SUMMER SCHOOL
YEAR BOOK

SHE WAS OKAY, I GUESS
...THUS THE LOVINGLY RENDERED HORNS, GOATEE, AND BLACKED-OUT TOOTH...
YEAR BOOK

JIM DAVIS 5-2
PLAY DEAD, ODIE!

GOOD BOY!

NOW, STAY

A WHAT?...ON YOUR **WHAT**?!

YES, MRS. FEENY. I'LL LOOK INTO IT

DEAD GERBIL ON HER GLIDER?!
NOT MY WORK. WAY TOO OBVIOUS

UH-OH

BAD SIGN

JON'S KITE CAME HOME WITHOUT HIM

GOOD COFFEE

HOT COFFEE
HERE IT COMES...

GOOOOOOOOD HOT COFFEE
SIGH

com

...AND TO YOUR RIGHT IS A HOUSE CAT. NOW LET'S MOVE TO THE LIVING ROOM

DO YOU FEEL A DRAFT?
YOU LEFT THE DOOR OPEN, DIPWAD

WHEN I LOOK AROUND THE ROOM AND SEE HOW DIRTY IT IS...

I THINK IT'S TIME WE DO SOMETHING ABOUT IT

GOT THE BLINDFOLDS RIGHT HERE
GIMME THE BLUE ONE
JIM DAVIS 5-7

I'M GOING TO MEDITATE
JIM DAVIS 5-8

YOU DO THAT

Z
I COULD USE A LITTLE MEDITATION MYSELF

WHO WANTS TO HAVE FUN?
JIM DAVIS 5-9

NOT ME! NOT ME!

MR. BALL OF YARN NEEDS SOME ATTENTION
YOU TWO HAVE A LOVELY LIFE TOGETHER

A GREAT NEW STORE OPENED UP, GARFIELD!

IT'S CALLED "CREATE-A-PET"

I NOW HAVE A BUNNY!
WHO MAIMS
JIM DAVIS 5-10

HEY, TINA, I'M THROWING A PARTY SATURDAY NIGHT. WANT TO COME?
JIM DAVIS 5-11

YEEES, I'LL BE THERE
PARTY POOPER

GARFIELD, WEEKENDS ARE MY TIME TO REAR BACK AND HOWL!
CLOSE

...LIE DOWN AND GIGGLE?
CLOSER

...CRAWL INTO A FETAL POSITION AND WHIMPER?
THERE YOU GO
JIM DAVIS 5-12

garfield

© 2001 PAWS, INC. All Rights Reserved.

JIM DAVIS
5·13
Distributed by Universal Press Syndicate

IF SLEEPING IS AN ART,
THEN I'M A MASTERPIECE

CLICK
(DRIVEL)

CLICK
(NONSENSE)

AT LAST!
(NONSENSICAL) DRIVEL

THIS IS ONE LONG MOVIE

IT'S GOING ON LIKE, FOREVER!

WHERE'S THE REMOTE?!
YOU'RE SITTING ON THE PAUSE BUTTON, TECHNO BOY

WELCOME TO "RECYCLE THAT ROADKILL." WHAT HAVE WE GOT TONIGHT, BOB?

HARD TO TELL, CHUCK... HE'S PRETTY FLAT...

MIGHT MAKE A NICE COASTER
WITH GREAT BIG EYES

AND YOUR AVOCATION, SIR, IS?
I SQUISH SPIDERS

CARE TO DEMONSTRATE?
CERTAINLY

SQUISH!
LOUSY FORM
NO FOLLOW-THROUGH AT ALL
JIM DAVIS 5-17

...WE DID HAVE SOME AMAZING FOOTAGE OF THAT DOWNTOWN FIRE, BUT DAN IN EDITING ACCIDENTALLY ERASED IT...
JIM DAVIS 5-18

SO, INSTEAD OF EXCITING FIRE FOOTAGE, WE PRESENT DAN IN HIS UNDERSHIRT AND BOXER SHORTS PLAYING A COMB WITH TISSUE PAPER:

FFFT
FFFT
FFFT
I'D TAKE THIS OVER A FIRE ANY OLD DAY

Z
Z
JIM DAVIS 5-19

Z
Z

THIS HAS BEEN "NAP ALONG WITH FLUFFY"
YAWN

GARFIELD, YOU SLEEP TOO MUCH
I HAVE A CONDITION

AND THERE'S A NAME FOR THAT
"EXERCISEOPHOBIA"

LAZY!
THE FEAR OF SWEAT

THERE WAS A COOKIE ON THIS PLATE A MINUTE AGO...
JIM DAVIS 5-25

AND I WANT TO KNOW WHERE IT WENT!

IT'S ENJOYING THE COMPANY OF THE MISSING PORK CHOP

THIS CAT FOOD CONTAINS TUNA-FLAVORED CHICKEN...
GARFIELD

THAT LOOKS LIKE BEEF
GARFIELD

I PREFER THE BEEF-FLAVORED TUNA THAT LOOKS LIKE CHICKEN
GARFIELD

GARFIELD

HOW'S IT GOING, GIANT HAMBURGER?

GIANT HAMBURGER?

YOU'RE DREAMING
THAT'S WHAT I ASSUMED

JIM DAVIS 5-27

NEVER ASSUME!

HERE ARE YOUR MENUS, HON
I LOVE DINERS

OOOH, I HAVE HEARTBURN ALREADY!
I'M IN DEEP-FRIED HEAVEN

HMM...THE THREE-BEAN BURRITO LOOKS GOOD...

SORRY, WE'RE OUT OF THAT
I OWE YOU ONE, IRMA

WOULD YOU LIKE EXTRA HORSERADISH SAUCE ON YOUR GARLIC-ONION-SARDINE SANDWICH?

SURE
NO GOODNIGHT KISS FOR YOU

THERE'S A NOTE IN MY SANDWICH

IT SAYS, "INSPECTED BY NUMBER 23"

THEY INSPECTED MY TUNA MELT?
THAT, OR THE COOK'S WEARING A NEW SHIRT

MY COMPLIMENTS TO THE CHEF!
I'LL TELL HIM

HE SAYS HE COULD USE A HUG
I HATED MY MEAL

AHHH...A FILLING MEAL AT A GREASY DINER
BURRRAAP

THEN HOME TO FALL ASLEEP ON THE COUCH IN FRONT OF THE T.V.!

CHECK!
IT JUST DOESN'T GET ANY BETTER THAN THIS

GARFIELD

ALMOST READY...

KACHING!
CLONK
MY EYE!

HOT! HOT!
HOT! HOT!
HOT! HOT!

SPLORT!

WAAAAH!
SCHLIIIP!

HERE'S YOUR TOAST
I THINK I'LL JUST HAVE A COLD BAGEL INSTEAD
JIM DAVIS 6-3

WAKE UP, GARFIELD!
JIM DAVIS 6-4

THE WHOLE WORLD IS WAITING FOR YOU!

TELL THE WORLD TO GET A LIFE

I REALLY SHOULD CUT THE GRASS... BUT IT'S SUCH A NICE DAY
JIM DAVIS 6-5

MAYBE I'LL WATER IT INSTEAD

WHAT'S WITH THE SUNGLASSES?
YOU'RE BLINDING ME WITH YOUR LOGIC

I THOUGHT ODIE WAS CHASING YOU AROUND THE TREE OUT BACK

HE IS

I DON'T THINK HE'S CAUGHT ME YET
JIM DAVIS 6-6

THERE WERE THREE DOZEN COOKIES ON THIS PLATE...

AND NOW THEY'RE GONE!

BAD PLATE!
JIM DAVIS 6-7

YOU KNOW, ODIE...

THE SECRET TO LOOKING GOOD IS TO ACCESSORIZE

JIM DAVIS 6-8

YOU KNOW, GARFIELD, I'M NOT REALLY BORING
JIM DAVIS 6-9

I'M MELLOW

I HAVE A LAID-BACK PERSONALITY
THAT'S WHY WE BURIED IT IN THE BACKYARD THREE YEARS AGO

GARFIELD

AH, THE SIMPLE, DIRECT APPROACH
BEWARE OF DOG

SELF-EXPLANATORY
BEWARE OF DUMB MUTT

HIGH-TECH MIXED BREED
BEWARE OF

NO THREAT THERE
Beware of Poochie

JiM DAViS 6-10

I BELIEVE WE HAVE A WINNER

YOU'D NEVER GUESS YOU WERE GOING TO BE 23. WHY, YOU'RE AS ACTIVE AS YOU EVER WERE

HA, HA, VERY FUNNY!

SO YOU'LL BE A YEAR OLDER... SO WHAT?

BIRTHDAYS ARE A CELEBRATION OF LIFE!

YEAH, WE CAN DECORATE YOUR WALKER WITH STREAMERS AND EVERYTHING!
WHO LET HIM IN?!!

GARFIELD, WILL YOU PLAY WITH ME?
GO AWAY, NERMAL

WE COULD RUN AND LAUGH!
GO AWAY, NERMAL

OR IN YOUR CASE, WADDLE AND WHEEZE
COME CLOSER, NERMAL

LOOK ON THE BRIGHT SIDE, GARFIELD...
JIM DAVIS 6-14

EVERY YEAR, YOUR BIRTHDAY IS A GIFT!
YEAH, YEAH

A GIFT WITH NO EXCHANGES OR RETURNS

I HEAR YOU HAVE A BIRTHDAY COMING UP... HOW OLD?
23

WHAT WOULD THAT BE IN SPIDER YEARS?
DON'T KNOW... NO SPIDER HAS EVER LIVED THAT LONG

WHOA, HOW IRONIC WAS THAT?
JIM DAVIS 6-15

INSTEAD OF MAKING A LIST OF THINGS I WANT FOR MY BIRTHDAY...

I MADE A LIST OF THINGS I DON'T WANT

RAISINS?
JIM DAVIS 6-16